Collins English Readers

Amazing Inventors

Level 1
CEF A2

Text by
Silvia Tiberio

Series edited by
Fiona MacKenzie

Collins

HarperCollins Publishers
77–85 Fulham Palace Road
Hammersmith London W6 8JB

10 9 8 7 6 5 4 3 2 1

Original text
© The Amazing People Club Ltd

Adapted text
© HarperCollins Publishers Ltd 2014

ISBN: 978-0-00-754494-3

Collins® is a registered trademark of
HarperCollins Publishers Limited

www.collinselt.com

A catalogue record for this book is available
from the British Library

Printed in the UK by Martins the Printers

These readers are based on original texts
(BioViews®) published by The Amazing
People Club group.® BioViews® and The
Amazing People Club® are registered
trademarks and represent the views of the
author.

BioViews® are scripted virtual interview
based on research about a person's life and
times. As in any story, the words are only
an interpretation of what the individuals
mentioned in the BioViews® could have
said. Although the interpretations are
based on available research, they do not
purport to represent the actual views of
the people mentioned. The interpretations
are made in good faith, recognizing that
other interpretations could also be made.
The author and publisher disclaim any
responsibility from any action that readers
take regarding the BioViews® for educational
or other purposes. Any use of the BioViews®
materials is the sole responsibility of the
reader and should be supported by their own
independent research.

Cover image © udra/Shutterstock

MIX
Paper from
responsible sources
FSC www.fsc.org FSC™ C007454

FSC™ is a non-profit international organisation established to promote the
responsible management of the world's forests. Products carrying the FSC
label are independently certified to assure consumers that they come from
forests that are managed to meet the social, economic and ecological needs
of present and future generations, and other controlled sources.

Find out more about HarperCollins and the environment at
www.harpercollins.co.uk/green

◆ CONTENTS ◆

Collins Amazing People Readers are collections of short stories. Each book presents the life story of five or six people whose lives and achievements have made a difference to our world today. The stories are carefully graded to ensure that you, the reader, will both enjoy and benefit from your reading experience.

You can choose to enjoy the book from start to finish or to dip in to your favourite story straight away. Each story is entirely independent.

After every story a short timeline brings together the most important events in each person's life into one short report. The timeline is a useful tool for revision purposes.

Words which are above the required reading level are underlined the first time they appear in each story. All underlined words are defined in the glossary at the back of the book. Levels 1 and 2 take their definitions from the *Collins COBUILD Essential English Dictionary* and levels 3 and 4 from the *Collins COBUILD Advanced English Dictionary*.

To support both teachers and learners, additional materials are available online at www.collinselt.com/readers.

The Amazing People Club®

Collins Amazing People Readers are adaptations of original texts published by The Amazing People Club. The Amazing People Club is an educational publishing house. It was founded in 2006 by educational psychologist and management leader Dr Charles Margerison and publishes books, eBooks, audio books, iBooks and video content which bring readers 'face to face' with many of the world's most inspiring and influential characters from the fields of art, science, music, politics, medicine and business.

◆ THE GRADING SCHEME ◆

The Collins COBUILD Grading Scheme has been created using the most up-to-date language usage information available today. Each level is guided by a brand new comprehensive grammar and vocabulary framework, ensuring that the series will perfectly match readers' abilities.

		CEF band	Pages	Word count	Headwords
Level 1	elementary	A2	64	5,000–8,000	approx. 700
Level 2	pre-intermediate	A2–B1	80	8,000–11,000	approx. 900
Level 3	intermediate	B1	96	11,000–15,000	approx. 1,100
Level 4	upper intermediate	B2	112	15,000–18,000	approx. 1,700

For more information on the Collins COBUILD Grading Scheme, including a full list of the grammar structures found at each level, go to www.collinselt.com/readers/gradingscheme.

Also available online: Make sure that you are reading at the right level by checking your level on our website (www.collinselt.com/readers/levelcheck).

Johannes Gutenberg

◆ ◆ ◆

*c.*1400–1468

the man who invented the printing press

I invented a machine to print books – the printing press. After my invention, books were cheaper and easier to make. Books <u>spread</u> ideas around the world. I started the information age. But during my life, no one <u>valued</u> my work.

◆ ◆ ◆

I went to school in Mainz, Germany. When I was young, there were very few books because it took several weeks to make just one copy. Books were written by hand, usually by <u>priests</u>. They wrote with a quill – a pen made from a bird's <u>feather</u> – and it wasn't always easy to read their handwriting. I asked myself, 'Can I invent a machine to put words on paper?' A machine can make more books in less time.

My training as a <u>goldsmith</u> gave me good ideas for a printing press. I started my <u>experiments</u> in Strasbourg in 1436. I had a girlfriend and we were engaged, but I didn't have very much money. So I couldn't get married and do my experiments as well. I had to choose – should I get married or continue my work on my printing press? It was so hard to decide that I couldn't sleep at night. Finally, after a lot of thinking, I told my girlfriend, 'I'm really sorry, but I can't get married. I need the money for my experiments.'

It was a difficult time. In my town, people had a bad opinion of me. My girlfriend was so angry that she took me to <u>court</u> because I broke my promise. And I was so poor that I had to borrow money to buy <u>materials</u> for my experiments.

In 1440, after four years of hard work, I invented a printing press that worked. It was a wooden press with 'movable type'. To make it work, I made small metal letters and put them in a wooden <u>block</u>. I used the same block to make several copies of the same page. My <u>system</u> was called 'movable type' because you could move the letters from one place in the block to another.

I was very pleased with my invention, but businessmen weren't interested in it. In 1444, I decided to open my own <u>workshop</u>. I printed some poems and in 1448, I printed the calendar for the year. I <u>earned</u> some money, but I couldn't pay off my <u>debts</u>.

Johannes Gutenberg's printing press

♦ ◆ ♦

In 1450, I met Johann Fust, a rich man who gave me 8,000 <u>guilders</u>. His daughter's husband, Peter Schöffer, started to work with me in my business. Soon my printing press was working again. I did some small jobs – for example, I printed some poems.

Next, I wanted to do something big, so I borrowed more money from Fust and printed the *Gutenberg <u>Bible</u>*. It was a very beautiful book with 42 lines per page. But the cost of making each bible was much higher than the money I got for selling it. Soon my money problems were much bigger than before. My debt was very big now – 20,000 guilders.

My <u>situation</u> was very bad, but things got worse when, in 1455, Fust took me to court. He said, 'Gutenberg borrowed some money from me to print books and used it to pay for other things!' This was not true, but to my surprise, he won the <u>case</u>!

In one day, I lost everything – my workshop, my machine and all my materials! The court gave them all to Fust. He used my printing press to open a new printing company with Schöffer. Without my machine, I couldn't work or pay off my debts.

After several years, I started printing again, but there was a lot of competition then. There were more than 100 printing companies in Germany and there were printing companies in France and Spain, too. And they all used my idea – the movable type system.

My machine changed the world, but no one thought my work was useful during my life. The printing press was a very important invention. With books, people could read and learn. With books, people could <u>share political</u> ideas and ideas about technology. My printing press started the information age.

The Life of Johannes Gutenberg

c.1400   Johannes Gutenberg was born in Mainz, Germany. He was the youngest son of a businessman.

1407   He went to school and learnt how to read and write.

1411   His family moved to Strasbourg.

1418   He studied at the University of Erfurt.

1420   He had a number of jobs. He worked as a goldsmith.

1430   He moved from Mainz to Strasbourg.

1434   He became a member of the Goldsmith's Guild.

1436   He began work on his printing press.

1437   He decided that he wasn't going to get married. His girlfriend took him to court.

1438   He borrowed money from Andreas Dritzehn to continue his experiments in printing.

1440   He invented the wooden press with movable type.

1444   He returned to Mainz and started a printing shop at Hof Humbrecht.

1446   He printed the *Poem of the Last Judgment*.

1448   He printed the calendar for 1448. He
       borrowed money from Arnold Gelthus. He
       was his sister's husband.

1450   He borrowed 8,000 guilders from Johann
       Fust. Peter Schöffer started working with
       Gutenberg.

1452   He borrowed 800 guilders from Fust. He
       began printing the *Gutenberg Bible*.

1455   He had a debt of 20,000 guilders. Fust took
       him to court.

1456   Fust won the case in court. He was given
       Gutenberg's printing workshop by the court.
       Gutenberg lost everything.

1459   Gutenberg opened a small printing shop.

1468   He died in Mainz, Germany. He was
       70 years old. At the time, no one thought
       his invention was important.

Louis
Braille

◆ ◆ ◆

1809–1852

the man who invented an alphabet for the blind

I became <u>blind</u> when I was a child. There were very few books for people who couldn't see. It was very difficult for us to learn how to read and write. We needed an easy <u>system</u>. Could I invent one?

◆ ◆ ◆

When I was a child, I was <u>curious</u>, like most boys. My father had a <u>workshop</u> and made <u>harnesses</u> for horses. He had a lot of <u>tools</u> that I was interested in. One day, I picked up an awl – a very sharp tool – from my father's table and I started playing with it. Suddenly, I tripped and fell. The awl hurt my eye badly. The doctor tried to help me, but my eye became <u>infected</u>. Soon my other eye became infected, too. I was 5 years old when I couldn't see the sun, the fields or the blue sky anymore.

We lived in Coupvray, a small town east of Paris. At school, I couldn't run or play with the other boys. It was difficult to learn because I couldn't read or write. My teacher and the local <u>priest</u> tried hard to teach me, but I didn't make much progress. I was slower than the other children in the class.

My parents were very worried about my future. They didn't want me to become a <u>beggar</u>. They wanted me to study. One day, my father heard of Quinze-Vingts, a school for blind people in Paris, and decided to take me there.

I was 10 years old and full of hope when I arrived at the school. 'Do you have books for a blind person?' was my first question to Doctor Guille, the doctor in charge of the school. I was pleased to hear that they had. 'This is the right place for me,' I thought. But soon I found out that life at Quinze-Vingts was very hard.

The school wasn't a pleasant place. The building was 500 years old and the rooms were cold and <u>damp</u>. And Doctor Guille wasn't a pleasant man. He was a <u>cruel</u> man who hit his students and used very unkind words to describe blind people. I was very upset.

At Quinze-Vingts, students weren't taught how to read or write. Doctor Guille wasn't interested in that. We were taught how to make baskets, chairs and <u>slippers</u>. For Doctor Guille, we weren't students. We were workers! He sold the beautiful things that we made! I was sad, lonely and a long way from home. My parents didn't know that my life was so hard.

Although the school was bad, it was the only place that had books for blind people. The books were large, heavy and expensive. The letters were <u>raised</u> from the page and I felt them with my fingers. The problem was that I took a very long time to read each word. When I got to the end of the sentence, I couldn't remember the beginning. But I wanted to read. There were 14 books in the school and I decided to read them all.

Things got better when, in 1821, Doctor Pignier became the director of the school. We started to have music lessons. I loved to play music and it became my favourite <u>hobby</u>. It was much easier than reading because I didn't need to read music. I could play by ear. I was asked to play at many <u>churches</u> in Paris. It was good to be outside the school. People said nice things to me. I was paid for my work and I had my own money for the first time in my life. This meant a lot to me.

◆ ◆ ◆

When I was 12 years old, Charles Barbier, who worked for the <u>army</u>, visited our school. He told us about the system that his army used to read in the dark. They couldn't use light because the enemy might see them, so they used a system with 12 <u>dots</u> and <u>dashes</u>. The system was difficult, but it gave me an idea.

When I returned home for a holiday, I started working on my idea. I went to my father's workshop and picked up an awl – the tool that hurt my eye – to invent a new system for reading and writing. I used the awl to raise dots on a page. Barbier's system had 12 symbols. My system was easier. It had only six. In 1824, I was 15 years old and I had a <u>basic</u> system. Five years later, the first book was <u>published</u>. It was called *Method of Writing Words and Music and Plain Songs by Means of Dots, for Use by the Blind and Arranged for Them*. The system was called the Braille System.

I was very happy with my system, but most teachers didn't want to use it. They weren't blind and they didn't need it. They preferred the old system with raised letters because they didn't want to learn something new. But I continued to use it and started to teach people to use it. In 1834, it was shown at an <u>exhibition</u> in Paris.

I became a teacher at my old school. My students made progress quickly and this made me very happy. But I was ill and I began to feel very weak. The damp conditions in the school weren't good for my health. The doctor said that I had <u>tuberculosis</u> and in 1844, I had to stop teaching.

But my students continued to use my system. And then, little by little, the system <u>spread</u> to other schools and other parts of the world. It became the reading and writing system for the blind. My students kept the Braille System <u>alive</u>!

The Life of Louis Braille

1809   Louis Braille was born in Coupvray, France.

1812   He had an accident with an awl and hurt one
       of his eyes. Both eyes became infected. He
       was 5 years old and he became blind.

1815   Father Jacques Palluy from the Coupvray
       Catholic church helped with Louis' education.

1819   Louis went to Paris to study at the Royal
       Institute for Blind Youth (Quinze-Vingts).

1821   Charles Barbier visited the school and talked
       about his system for reading in the dark.
       Louis had the idea to invent his own system.

1824   He showed his work to Doctor Pignier, the
       Director at the National Institute for Blind
       Youth.

1826   He finished school and became an assistant
       teacher at the same school.

1828   He became a teacher.

1829   He published his book *Method of Writing
       Words, Music and Plain Songs by Means of
       Dots, for Use by the Blind and Arranged for
       Them.*

1834   He showed his system at the Paris Exhibition of Industry.

1835   He became ill with tuberculosis.

1837   The second edition of the Braille system was published.

1843   The Royal Institute for Blind Youth was moved to a better building.

1844   Louis stopped teaching.

1852   Louis died of tuberculosis when he was 43 years old.

Alexander Graham Bell

♦ ♦ ♦

1847–1922

the man who invented the telephone

**I was always interested in sounds. My mother
was <u>deaf</u> and my father taught deaf people. I was
<u>creative</u> and enjoyed inventing things. I did a lot of
<u>experiments</u> and one day, I invented the telephone.**

◆ ◆ ◆

I was born in Edinburgh, Scotland. When I was a child,
I liked to learn new things. I liked art, poems and music,
and I could play the piano very well.

I invented my first machine when I was 12 years old. I
had a friend and his father had a <u>mill</u>. One day, we were
playing together in the mill, when my friend's father
told us, 'Why don't you do something useful?' 'That's a
good idea,' I thought, and I invented a new machine. My
friend's father was very surprised. The machine could

separate the outside parts of <u>wheat grains</u> from the inside parts. The machine could do the job quickly and easily.

I left school when I was 15 years old because I wasn't interested in school lessons. My father was worried about my decision because he thought education was very important. He was a professor at Edinburgh University and worked on 'Visible Speech', a <u>system</u> to teach deaf people.

I was interested in my father's work, maybe because my mother was deaf. One day, I read a book that gave me an idea – that it was possible to use electricity to produce sound. I decided to work on that.

◆ ◆ ◆

But hard times came. Between 1867 and 1870, two of my brothers became ill with <u>tuberculosis</u> and died. I also became ill and I was very weak. My father thought that our family needed a new start and one day, he made a decision. 'We're going to move to Canada,' he said.

I was 23 years old when we sailed across the Atlantic Ocean. When we were there, my father bought a farmhouse in Ontario. Life on the farm was good for my health and it helped me feel stronger. In Ontario, I met the Indians from the Six Nations Reserve, learnt their language and used my father's system to help the deaf people in their <u>community</u>. They were so happy that they named me <u>honorary chief</u>. To celebrate, I put on their clothes and danced. It was great fun!

In 1871, my father and I started teaching deaf people in Montreal. My father was such a good teacher that he received an invitation to work in Boston in the USA. We travelled there and opened a school to train teachers of the deaf. Suddenly, my life became very busy. I spent six months in Boston and the rest at home in Ontario. I started my <u>research</u> on sounds and electricity. I did most of my research on my own at night and I was so tired that I often had terrible headaches. In 1875, when Thomas Watson became my assistant, I finally got some help.

◆ ◆ ◆

One day, I met a man who was very important in my life. His name was Antonio Meucci. He showed me his invention, a <u>basic</u> telephone with one <u>line</u> to carry <u>signals</u>. His invention gave me an idea. Soon I started doing experiments to invent a telephone with more than one line.

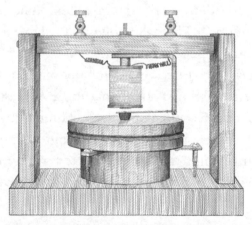

Bell's first telephone

On 2ⁿᵈ June 1875, my telephone worked for the first time. I was at one end of the line in one room and Watson was at the other end of the line in another room. 'Watson. Come here. I want to see you.' And Watson came to see me! This was the start of a <u>revolution</u> that changed the world. I got a <u>patent</u> for my telephone. It was patent number 174,465.

After that, I decided to work hard on my new invention. I didn't have much time to work as a teacher, so I only had two students and one of them was Mabel Hubbard. Mabel was deaf, but she could read your lips and speak, and she later became my wife. Her father was a friend of mine.

Mr Hubbard was interested in my work and gave me money for my experiments. With his help, I invented a new telephone that could send messages more than five miles. I offered it to the company Western Union, but their president said it was a toy. The American government said, 'This telephone isn't useful. And it will be dangerous in people's homes.'

I decided to start my own company without help from businessmen or the government. In 1877, I started the Bell Telephone Company with Mr Hubbard. In 1881, I started the Volta <u>Laboratory</u> in Washington and invented many useful things. In 1885, I started a new company. I had a very busy life. I was a <u>successful</u> inventor and businessman!

The Life of Alexander Graham Bell

1847   Alexander Bell was born in Edinburgh, Scotland.

1858   His father gave him the middle name of 'Graham' on his 11th birthday.

c.1859   He built a machine that could separate the outside parts of wheat grains from the inside parts. He became interested in 'Visible Speech', a system that his father used for helping deaf people.

1867   His brother, Edward, died of tuberculosis. Alexander became ill.

1870   His brother, Melville, also died of tuberculosis. The Bell family moved to Canada. He and his father later opened a school in Boston, USA.

1873   Mabel Hubbard, his future wife, became his student. She was the daughter of Gardiner Greene Hubbard.

1875   Thomas Watson became his assistant. Bell's telephone worked for the first time.

1876   He got a patent for a telephone that could send a message more than five miles.

1877   He formed the Bell Telephone Company. He married Mabel Hubbard and they moved to the UK for 15 months. They later had two daughters and two sons.

1881   He invented the metal detector – an instrument to find metal. He started the Volta Laboratory in Washington. He invented many useful things in this laboratory.

1882   He became American.

1885   He started the American Telephone and Telegraph Company.

1888   The National Geographic Society was formed. He was one of the founding fathers.

1890   He started the American Association to Promote Teaching Speech to the Deaf.

1909   His plane, Silver Dart, was able to fly.

1915   He made the first telephone call from one side of America to the other. Alexander was in New York and he talked on the telephone with his assistant, Watson, in San Francisco.

1919   Alexander and Casey Baldwin invented the HD-4 hydroplane – a fast boat that travelled on the surface of the water. It was the fastest hydroplane at the time.

1922   Alexander died in Nova Scotia, Canada. He was 75 years old.

Thomas Edison

◆ ◆ ◆

1847–1931

the man who invented the electric light bulb

One day, I was poor. The next, I was rich. I brought light to cities and invented lots of new things. How did I do it? I worked hard. But I also had good luck. I met the right people at the right time.

♦ ◆ ♦

I was born in the United States. I went to school for only three months because my teacher thought that I caused <u>trouble</u> in the classroom. In fact, I spoke in a loud voice because I couldn't hear very well. When I left school, I was only 7 years old. My mother became my teacher at home.

My parents had seven children and I was the youngest. We didn't have much money, so when I was 12 years old, all my brothers and sisters worked. I decided to work too. I got a job on the railways and I sold food and drinks on trains.

One day, I was at Mount Clemens station when I saw a little boy on the railway. There was a train coming and I ran to save him. The boy was the <u>stationmaster's</u> 3-year-old son. He wanted to thank me for saving his son and taught me how to use the <u>telegraph</u>. I could get a better job now!

◆ ◆ ◆

From 1863 to 1867, I worked as a telegraph operator. I liked machines and I sometimes did <u>experiments</u>. When I was 19, I had a job at The Western Union Company in Louisville. One day, I was trying an experiment when I <u>spilt</u> <u>acid</u> in the office and lost my job. I moved to Boston and invented a machine to record <u>votes</u>. No one was interested in it, so when I was 22 years old, I decided to go to New York to make a new start.

I knew one person in New York so I went to see him. 'I haven't got a job and I need some money. Could I borrow some from you?' I asked. He was surprised. 'I can only lend you a dollar,' he said. I took the dollar and promised to give it back. This dollar changed my life.

I was hungry and weak, so I used the dollar to buy a meal. I felt much stronger after my meal and I went out to look for a job. I talked to a few people. One of them was Franklin Pope. He worked for The Gold Indicator Company and he showed me the company's building. I stayed in the <u>battery</u> room that night. The next day, I studied the company's machines. The third day was my lucky day.

There was a machine that sent important information to the Gold Exchange. Suddenly, it stopped working. The people in the company didn't know what to do. But I knew what to do. I <u>repaired</u> the machine. Doctor Samuel Laws, from the Gold Exchange, heard of my work. He offered to pay me $300 a month to repair their machines! I was able to pay the dollar back.

Soon the president of the Gold and Stock Telegraph Company also heard of my work. 'Can you repair the machines in our company?' he asked me. $3,000 or $5,000 a year was good pay for the job, but he offered me $40,000! I was lucky once again.

♦ ◆ ♦

This was the start of my <u>career</u> as a businessman and inventor. I moved to New Jersey and I opened several telegraph companies with Franklin Pope. In 1870, Mary Stilwell got a job in one of my companies. We got married the next year and had three children. I was happy to have a family but I didn't have much time to be at home. I had a lot of ideas for new inventions. In 1876, I built a <u>research laboratory</u> at Menlo Park, formed a team and invented the phonograph – a machine to play music – and many other things.

Thomas Edison's research laboratory

My most important invention came next. Every day when the sun set, everything was dark. We had electricity but we had no electric light. After a lot of experiments and hours of hard work at the laboratory, we invented the electric light bulb – the round, glass object that produces light. In 1882, I helped to put 400 lights in the streets of Manhattan. New York got a new name, 'The City That Never Sleeps'. I brought light to homes, hospitals, offices, factories and schools. It was the beginning of the 24-7 lifestyle – 24 hours of light, seven days a week.

Then, a sad day arrived in my life. In 1884, my wife became ill and died. But two years later, I got married to Mina Miller and had three children. At work, it was a time of <u>success</u>. I started more companies and invented more things. I got one <u>patent</u> every ten days. There were 1,093 in total!

Then hard times came again. In 1913, a big fire <u>destroyed</u> 13 of our buildings. The next year, the First World War started in Europe. The government asked me to work on inventions to find <u>guns</u> and <u>submarines</u>. I couldn't work on my inventions anymore.

During my life, I started a lot of companies and invented many things. One day, I was asked, 'How did you do it?' My answer was, 'One per cent <u>inspiration</u> and 99 per cent <u>perspiration</u>'. Hard work was the key.

The Life of Thomas Edison

1847   Thomas Alva Edison was born in Ohio, USA.

1859   When he was 12 years old, he worked on the railways. He sold food and drinks. A few years later, he produced a newspaper, the *Grand Trunk Herald*.

1862   The stationmaster's son was playing on the railway and Edison saved his life. The stationmaster taught him how to use the telegraph.

1863–1867   He travelled between cities. He worked as a telegraph operator on the Grand Trunk Railway in Ontario and for The Western Union Company. He moved to Louisville, Kentucky.

1868   He moved to Boston. He got a patent for the Electric Vote Recorder.

1869   He moved to New York. He got his first important job at Gold and Stock Telegraph Company. He started work as a businessman and inventor.

1870   He opened Newark Telegraph in New Jersey. He got a patent for the Universal Stock Ticker – a machine that printed telegraph messages.

1871   He married Mary Stilwell. They later had three children.

1874   He invented the electric pen and a copying machine.

1876   He opened the first industrial research laboratory in Menlo Park, New Jersey. In this laboratory, they did research on making things in factories.

1877   He invented the phonograph.

1879   He invented the light bulb.

1880   He started the Edison Illuminating Company.

1882   He helped to put 400 lights in the streets of Manhattan.

1883   He started the Edison & Swan United Electric Light Company.

1884   His wife died.

1886   He married Mina Miller. They later had three children.

1891   He made several inventions to improve electric railways. He formed Edison General Electric.

1900   He began work on an alkaline storage battery – a new, lighter and stronger battery.

1913   He invented a machine to add sound to films. A big fire destroyed 13 of Edison's buildings.

1915–1918   During the First World War, he worked on inventions to find submarines and guns.

1931   He died in his home in New Jersey. He was 84 years old.

Guglielmo Marconi

◆ ◆ ◆

1874–1937

the man who invented the wireless system

I invented the radio and sent the first <u>wireless</u> messages across the Atlantic. My invention changed the <u>speed</u> of communication. I also invented <u>radar</u> <u>systems</u>. They tell us the speed, position and direction of objects which we can't see.

◆ ◆ ◆

I was born in Italy. My mother was Irish and my father was Italian. When I was a child, I learnt two languages – English and Italian. I could communicate with people in two different ways. Communication was very important in my life.

When I was young, it wasn't easy to communicate with other countries. A few people used the <u>telegraph</u>. This machine sent electric <u>signals</u> through a <u>wire</u> between two places. I asked myself, 'Is there a better way to communicate?' 'Can one person hear another person at a distance without using a wire?' 'Can voice messages travel from one city to another?'

I wanted to find answers to my questions so I started doing <u>experiments</u>. I didn't attend university. I worked at home with very simple equipment and my father helped me. In 1895, I was able to send <u>radio waves</u> over a distance of 100 metres! I was very excited. But some scientists told me, 'It's only possible to send waves in straight lines.' They also said, 'It isn't possible if there is an object between the two places.' I didn't agree and I decided to try a new experiment.

I built a receiving station behind a hill and asked my assistant, Mr Mignani, to stay behind the hill. I gave him a <u>gun</u> and said, 'I'll send you a message from home. <u>Fire</u> this gun if you can hear me.' I went to my father's house and sent him the message. Suddenly, I heard a very loud sound. It was Mignani's gun! My <u>discovery</u> was very important because it was the first wireless radio message in history!

♦ ◆ ♦

I needed money for my <u>research</u> but in Italy no one was interested in my invention. I travelled to England in 1896 and showed my radio to William Preece from the British Post Office. He was interested in my work and decided to help me. He gave me money and I did many more experiments. Soon I was able to send messages over longer distances. My invention was now ready to use.

The next year, I got a <u>patent</u> for wireless telegraphy and started the Wireless Telegraph and Signal Company. More and more people from business and government showed interest in my work and my life became busier and busier. In 1898, I opened the first radio factory in England with the help of some <u>investors</u>. In 1899, radio communication between England and France became possible. My company was growing fast and we needed more people to work in the factory. As a result, a new training college was opened in 1901. It was an exciting time.

◆ ◆ ◆

My next question was, 'Can radio waves cross the Atlantic?' 'That's too far away,' many scientists said. Once again, I thought they were wrong so I tried a new experiment.

I sailed across the Atlantic to Newfoundland in Canada. When I was there, I put <u>antennae</u> on <u>kites</u>. The kites went high in the sky and helped to receive radio waves. On 12th December 1901, I got a message from Poldhu in England about 2,500 miles away. On that day, the world became smaller. The speed of communication did not <u>depend on</u> winds and ocean waves any more. It now depended on radio waves.

I was very lucky when I met Beatrice O'Brien. We got married on 16th March 1905, and we had three daughters and a son. It was a busy time. I was invited to Canada and Russia and received a lot of <u>honours</u>. In 1909, I received the Nobel Prize for Physics which I <u>shared</u> with Karl Braun.

In the same year, two ships, the *SS Republic* and the *SS Florida* <u>collided</u> in the North Atlantic Ocean. <u>Rescuers</u> received radio messages and saved 4,000 people from the ships. Three years later, 712 <u>survivors</u> of the *RMS Titanic* were saved because of wireless technology. My radio system helped to save lives!

◆ ◆ ◆

Soon everyone thought that my invention was very important. Communication did not depend on <u>undersea</u> wires or <u>landlines</u> any longer. My radio made communication much easier. Radio was useful for business, politics and wars, and I continued to work hard.

But sadly, the First World War started in 1914. Communication became so important that the British government took control of my company. I couldn't run my business or do research, so I decided to return to Italy. I joined the <u>army</u> and was <u>responsible</u> for the army's radio service. They were sad times. A lot of people died.

After the war, I returned to England because there was more opportunity to do business there. But I had to spend a lot of time in meetings. There was a strong connection between technology, power and business, and important people in business and government wanted to talk to me. I couldn't spend much time with my family. Our marriage ended in 1924.

I was very happy when, some years later, I met Maria Cristina Bezzi-Scali. We got married on 15th June 1927 and had a daughter three years later. I had a family again.

◆ ◆ ◆

During times of <u>peace</u>, I found more uses for wireless technology. People had radios in their homes. Ships used special radio waves. But my most important invention of the time was a new *Radio Detection and Ranging* system. It was called radar. Its waves could tell us the speed of objects. They could also tell us the exact position of planes and ships. I sold radar systems to different companies and governments around the world.

When I became ill, I decided to return to Italy. I wanted to spend the last years of my life in my country. I died in Rome in 1937. I made an important <u>contribution</u> to the world. I hope scientists will continue to develop wireless technology. I hope they will use it for the <u>benefit</u> of everyone.

The Life of Guglielmo Marconi

1874   Guglielmo Marconi was born in Bologna, Italy.

1895   He sent radio waves from his father's house to a small receiving station behind a hill.

1896   He travelled to London to show his invention. William Preece from the British Post Office showed interest. He gave his first public talk in London. It was called 'Telegraphy without Wires'.

1897   He got his first patent for wireless telegraphy. He started The Wireless Telegraph and Signal Company.

1898   He opened the world's first radio factory in Chelmsford, England.

1899   He sent a radio signal across the English Channel from France to England.

1900   His company changed its name to Marconi's Wireless Telegraph Company.

1901   He sent a message by radio telegraph across the Atlantic. He started Marconi's Wireless Telegraph Training College to teach people to use radio systems.

1905   He married Beatrice O'Brien. They had three daughters and a son.

1907   The Trans-Atlantic radio telegraph system started working.

1909   He received the Nobel Prize for Physics, together with Karl Braun, for their work on wireless telegraphy.

1912   His wireless technology helped to rescue survivors of the *RMS Titanic*.

1914   He joined the Italian army during the First World War. He was responsible for the army's radio service.

1920   He sent the first entertainment radio messages in the United Kingdom from the Chelmsford factory.

1922   He helped to start the British Broadcasting Company.

1924   He divorced his first wife.

1927   He married Maria Cristina Bezzi-Scali. They had a daughter, Maria Elettra Elena Anna, three years later.

1934   He continued his research and invented Radio Detection and Ranging (RADAR).

1937   He became ill and moved to Italy. He died when he was 63 years old in Rome. Radio stations around the world were silent for two minutes.

John Logie Baird

◆ ◆ ◆

1888–1946

the man who invented the television

I had an <u>illness</u> when I was a child and I had to live a quiet life. Technology became my <u>hobby</u>. We could send voice messages. Could I invent a <u>system</u> for sending pictures? I decided to try to do it.

◆ ◆ ◆

I had a serious illness when I was two years old and I couldn't do sport. I began to play with technical things. I had a friend who lived across the road and I built a phone that connected his home with mine. We sent messages to each other and had great fun. I was 12 years old at the time.

At school, I wasn't a very good student. 'He doesn't learn very quickly,' my teacher told my mother. But I worked hard and finished school. Then I entered university to study <u>electrical engineering</u>, but I couldn't finish my studies because the First World War started.

My health was poor, so I didn't fight during the war. I worked as an engineer at Clyde Valley Electricity in Glasgow. My job was to <u>repair</u> the machines there. But I wasn't interested in repairing things. I was interested in making them. I enjoyed doing <u>experiments</u>. One day, one of my experiments went wrong and the lights went out in some parts of Glasgow. I lost my job!

◆ ◆ ◆

I decided to try a new place and a new way of life. In 1919, I travelled to the island of Trinidad in the West Indies. Life was quiet on the island. The weather was so sunny that I felt much better there. I started new experiments with sounds and pictures. My neighbours heard strange noises in my house. They also saw lights that turned on and off. 'He's doing some kind of magic,' they thought. The local people were afraid of me. After a year on the island, I decided that Trinidad wasn't the best place for my experiments and I sailed back to England.

I asked myself, 'We have cameras to take pictures. We have radios to send messages. Is it also possible to send pictures?' I wanted to invent a system for sending <u>images</u> from one place to another and I started to work on my system. My first invention was a <u>basic</u> machine. I did more experiments and on 2nd October 1925, I showed my television in Selfridges, a large store in London. It was the first public presentation of my experiment. In 1927, I started a company – Baird Television Limited. I also got a <u>patent</u> for my invention and sent television images over 438 miles. It was a very exciting time.

♦ ◆ ♦

I borrowed some money and did more experiments. My television became better each day. In 1930, people could watch the first play on television. The next year, they could watch a horse <u>race</u> – the Derby. I did many things in a short period of time. But I also had a big <u>debt</u>. My company sold 10,000 televisions in the UK, but I needed to sell more televisions. I wanted to pay off my debt.

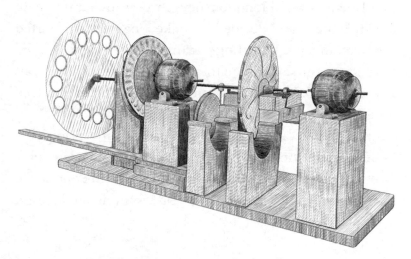

A part of Baird's first television

In 1931, I received an invitation to visit the USA. I sailed there with my girlfriend – and future wife – Margaret Albu. I knew that I could sell a lot of televisions in the USA but there was a <u>depression</u> at the time. In the UK, the <u>situation</u> wasn't any better. In 1936, the British Broadcasting Corporation (the BBC) didn't choose my system to send television programmes. Then the Second World War started in 1939. It was a very difficult time for my company.

During the war, London wasn't a safe place to live so I moved my family to Cornwall. I stayed in London because I had to work for the government. I had to help with the use of <u>radar</u> systems and secret <u>codes</u> and messages. There were many difficult days during the war and I made several long journeys to visit my family.

After the war, I decided to make a new start. I started a new company, John Logie Baird Limited, and worked very long hours. I wanted to invent colour television. But my health wasn't good and in 1946, I had a heart attack and I never recovered.

The television was a very important invention that changed education and <u>entertainment</u>. It changed people's lives. A lot of people use my invention. Think about the number of people around the world who watch television every day!

The Life of John Logie Baird

1888   John Logie Baird was born in Helensburgh, Scotland.

1900   When he was 12 years old, he built his own telephone.

1903   He read a German book about selenium – a chemical substance that he later used in his experiments. His interest in television began.

1914   He studied electrical engineering at Glasgow University. The First World War started. He stopped his studies. He started work for Clyde Valley Electricity.

1919   He went to Trinidad in the West Indies. He continued with his research and experiments there.

1920   He returned to England and started doing his research again.

1923–1924   His television showed the first moving pictures of objects.

1925   He showed the first human face on television at Selfridges in London. A year later, he showed the first moving pictures of objects at the Royal Institution in London.

1927   He sent a signal between London and
        Glasgow. He started Baird Television
        Limited.

1928–1930   He showed new kinds of television. He sent
             an image of a human face between UK and
             the USA. The first British Television Play on
             the BBC was transmitted: *The Man with the
             Flower in his Mouth.*

1931   He visited the USA and married a South
        African woman, Margaret Albu, in New
        York. They later had two children.

1932   By this year, the UK had sold 10,000
        television sets.

1936   The BBC chose the technology of
        Marconi–EMI for television programmes.
        This technology replaced John Baird's
        system.

1940   He did research on technical developments
        during the Second World War.

1944   He showed the first colour images on
        television. He continued with his research
        on colour television.

1946   He died when he was 57 years old in Sussex,
        England.

✦ GLOSSARY ✦

acid NOUN
a chemical, usually a liquid, that can burn your skin and cause damage to other substances

alive ADJECTIVE
continuing to exist or function

antenna (antennae or **antennas)** NOUN
a piece of equipment that sends and receives television or radio signals

army NOUN
a large group of soldiers who are trained to fight battles on land

basic ADJECTIVE
simple and not having many different functions or special features

battery NOUN
an object that provides electricity for things such as radios, or for computer systems if the main power system fails

beggar NOUN
someone who lives by asking people for money or food

benefit
for the benefit of someone in order to help someone improve their life

bible NOUN
the sacred book of the Christian religion

blind ADJECTIVE
unable to see
the blind people who are blind

block NOUN
a large, solid piece of a substance that has straight sides

career NOUN
a job that you do for a long time, or the years of your life that you spend working

case NOUN
a trial in a court at which people decide whether someone is guilty of a crime

chief NOUN
the leader of a group

church NOUN
a building where Christians go to pray

code NOUN
a secret way to replace the words in a message with other words or symbols, so that some people will not understand the message

collide VERB
to crash into another person or vehicle

community NOUN
a group of people who live in a particular area

contribution NOUN
something you do that helps achieve something or helps make it successful

court
to take someone to court to take legal action against someone

creative ADJECTIVE
good at having new ideas

cruel ADJECTIVE
deliberately making people suffer

curious ADJECTIVE
wanting to know more about something or about things in general

damp ADJECTIVE
having slight moisture in the air or on the walls

dash NOUN
a short, straight, horizontal line that you use in writing

deaf ADJECTIVE
unable to hear

debt NOUN
an amount of money that you owe someone

depend on PHRASAL VERB
to need someone or something in order to do something

depression NOUN
a time when there is very little economic activity so that a lot of people do not have jobs

destroy VERB
to cause so much damage to something that it cannot be used any longer, or does not exist any longer

discovery NOUN
something that someone finds or becomes aware of that no one knew about before

dot NOUN
a very small round mark, like the one on the letter 'i' or in the names of websites

earn VERB
to receive money for work that you do

electrical engineering
UNCOUNTABLE NOUN
the job or activity of designing
and building electrical devices

entertainment UNCOUNTABLE NOUN
plays, films and shows that
people watch for pleasure

exhibition NOUN
a public event where art or
interesting objects are shown

experiment NOUN
a scientific test that you do in
order to discover what happens
to something

feather NOUN
one of the light soft things that
cover a bird's body

fire VERB
to shoot a gun or a bullet

goldsmith NOUN
someone whose job is making
jewellery and other objects using
gold

grain NOUN
a single seed from a particular
crop

guilder NOUN
a unit of money that was used in
the Netherlands in the past

gun NOUN
a weapon that shoots bullets

harness NOUN
a set of straps that fits around
an animal, for example to attach
a piece of equipment to it

hobby NOUN
an activity that you enjoy doing
in your free time

honorary ADJECTIVE
having a title as a mark of
respect, rather than qualifying
for it in the normal way

honour NOUN
a special award that is given to
someone

illness NOUN
a particular disease or a period
of bad health

image NOUN
a picture of someone or
something

infected ADJECTIVE
affected by germs or bacteria

inspiration UNCOUNTABLE NOUN
a feeling of enthusiasm and new
ideas that you get from someone
or something

investor NOUN
a person or organization that
gives or lends money in the hope
of making a profit

kite NOUN
a toy that you fly in the wind at the end of a long string

laboratory NOUN
a building or a room where scientific work is done

landline NOUN
a wire that carries an electrical signal over land

line NOUN
a very long wire for telephones or electricity

materials PLURAL NOUN
the things that you need for a particular activity

mill NOUN
a building in which flour is made from grain

patent NOUN
an official right to be the only person or company to make and sell a new product

peace UNCOUNTABLE NOUN
a situation where there is not a war

perspiration UNCOUNTABLE NOUN
the liquid that appears on your skin when you are hot

political ADJECTIVE
relating to politics or the government

priest NOUN
a person who has religious duties in a place where people worship

publish VERB
to prepare and print copies of a book, a magazine or a newspaper

race NOUN
a competition to see who is the fastest

radar NOUN
a way of discovering the position of objects when they cannot be seen, by using radio signals

radio wave NOUN
the form in which radio signals travel

raise VERB
to move something upwards

repair VERB
to fix something that has been damaged or is not working properly

rescuer NOUN
someone who saves people from a dangerous situation

research UNCOUNTABLE NOUN
the work of studying something and trying to discover facts about it

responsible ADJECTIVE
having the job or duty to deal
with something

revolution NOUN
an important change in a
particular area of activity

share VERB
to exchange information,
opinions or ideas with someone

signal NOUN
a series of changes in electrical
current that may carry
information

situation NOUN
what is happening in a particular
place at a particular time

slipper NOUN
a loose, soft shoe that you wear
indoors

speed NOUN
how fast something moves or
is done

spill (spills, spilling, spilled or
spilt) VERB
to accidentally make a liquid flow
over the edge of a container

spread VERB
to make something gradually
reach a larger area

stationmaster NOUN
the person who is in charge of a
railway station

submarine NOUN
a type of ship that can travel
below the surface of the sea

success UNCOUNTABLE NOUN
when you do well and get the
result that you wanted

successful ADJECTIVE
doing or getting what you
wanted

survivor NOUN
someone who continues to live
after an accident or illness in
spite of almost dying

system NOUN
a way of doing something that
follows a fixed series of actions
or rules

telegraph NOUN
a machine for sending messages
over long distances by means of
electricity or radio signals, used
before the invention of
telephones

tool NOUN
anything that you hold in your
hands and use to do a particular
type of work

trouble UNCOUNTABLE NOUN
problems or difficulties

tuberculosis UNCOUNTABLE NOUN
a serious infectious disease that
affects the lungs

undersea ADJECTIVE
existing or happening below the
surface of the sea

value VERB
to think that something or
someone is important

vote NOUN
a choice made by a particular
person or group in a meeting or
an election

wheat UNCOUNTABLE NOUN
a crop that is grown for food. It
is made into flour and used for
making bread.

wire NOUN
a long thin piece of metal that
carries electricity

wireless ADJECTIVE
using radio waves instead
of wires

workshop NOUN
a place where people make or
repair things